The Unofficial Harry Potter Muggles To Magic Cookbook

by Gina Meyers

Serendipity Press books may be ordered online or by contacting:
Serendipity Media Group, LLC
P.O. Box 26734
Fresno, Ca. 93729
http://serendipitypressinc.blogspot.com/
serendipitypressinc@gmail.com
serendipitymediagroup@gmail.com

978-09825039-5-9

Book front and back cover concept and design by David Lawrence Meyers.
Photo Credit for Lemon Scones, Lauren Meyers. Photos credit for all other recipes, Gina Meyers. Editor and creative consultant, Liz Longo.

The Unofficial
Harry Potter Muggles To
Magic Cookbook

By Gina Meyers
Serendipity Media Press
California

Smuggle in some muggle magic with *The Unofficial Harry Potter Muggles To Magic Cookbook.* Inside this new and improved edition of *The Unofficial Harry Potter Cookbook: From Cauldron Cakes To Butterbeer*, you will find all things sugary to satisfy your sweet tooth, including Ron's Love Spell Sugar Cookies, Butterbeer Cupcakes, Pumpkin Juice, Hermiome's Precious Potion, Mulled Mead, Rock Cakes, Treacle Crisp, Pumpkin Fudge, Yorkshire Pudding, Cauldron Cakes, King's Cross Butterscotch Bars, Harry's Tea and Get Out Of a Jam Cookies, Cockroach Clusters, and much, much more, if you dare. With *The Unofficial Harry Potter Muggles To Magic*, you will conjure up easy to follow recipes that have been thoroughly researched and taste tested. Harry Potter fans will delight in recreating their favorite delicacies so smuggle in some muggle magic and try your hand or magic wand at Potter Stew, Hogwarts Best Bruscetta, Lasagna, Banoffi Inspired Pizza Pie, Christmas Coconut Soup, Dumbledore's Delightful Dumplings, and much, much more.

Table of Contents

Hogwarts, Hogwarts, Hoggy Warty Hogwarts
Teach us something, please
Whether we be old and bald
Or young with scabby knees,
Our heads could do with filling
With some interesting stuff.
For now they're bare and full of air
Dead flies and bits of fluff.
So teach us things worth knowing
Bring back what we've forgot.
Just do your best, we'll do the rest,
And learn until our brains all rot.

Sweet Treat From Mrs. Weasley

1 ¾ cups of Graham cracker crumbs
½ cup granulated sugar
¾ cup margarine, melted
¾ cup all-purpose flour
½ cup of coconut

Filling
½ cup of granulated sugar
1 egg
1 cup of lemon juice, plus ¼ tsp. of lemon rind
½ cup of shredded coconut

Directions: Melt the margarine and pour over the first ingredients.
Combine in a large bowl and work together until crumbly. Press

the mixture into an ungreased 9x9 inch pan and set aside. Next, place filling ingredients in a pot on low heat, stirring until thickened. Pour filling over bottom layer. Cook for 25 minutes in a 350 degree over. Depending on the size you cut for the squares, makes approximately 30 squares.

Chamber of Secrets Snack

2 7-inch flour tortillas
2 tablespoons strawberry cream cheese
¼ cup of raisins
¼ cup of dried cranberries
1 cup finely chopped green apples
1 teaspoon sugar and cinnamon combined

Directions: Finely chop apples and place them in a medium sized bowl. Add cranberries, raisins, and sugar cinnamon mixture and stir. Then, fry the tortilla with one tablespoon of margarine in a skillet till crisp. Place tortilla on a paper towel to take off excess margarine and to cool. Once cooled, spread cream cheese and top with apple concoction.

Ants on a Log

Celery stock
Peanut butter, smooth kind
Raisins

Directions: Break off a celery stock, wash and dry it. With a knife, or plastic spoon, spread peanut butter onto the celery stock. Top the peanut butter with raisins (black ants) or dried cranberries (red ants).

Pumpkin Fudge

3 cups sugar
¾ cups margarine
½ cup of evaporated milk
½ cup of pumpkin pie filling
1 package of white chocolate chips
1 jar of marshmallow cream
1 teaspoon of vanilla extract
1 tablespoon of pumpkin pie spice

Directions: Stir together the sugar, margarine, evaporated milk and pumpkin pie filling in a sauce pan. Bring to a boil, stirring constantly. Remove from heat, and add in the chocolate chips until they are melted. Mix the remaining ingredients until well blended. Pour into a greased 9x9 inch pan. Cool. Cut into squares. May wrap in colored saran wrap. Fudge keeps best when wrapped in waxed paper or individually in saran wrap.

Rock Cakes

½ cup of margarine
3/4 cup of confectioner's sugar (powdered sugar)
1 tablespoon of vanilla extract
1 ½ cups of flour
1/8 teaspoon of salt
Food coloring-optional
Chocolate pieces, peanut butter chips, nuts, cherries.

Directions: Heat oven to 350 degrees. Thoroughly mix together margarine, vanilla, sugar, and three drops of food coloring (any color). Add flour and salt and work until dough can hold together. Mold dough by Tablespoonfuls around a few chocolate pieces, nuts, or cherries. Place cookie dough on a baking sheet approximately 1 inch apart for 10 minutes or until light brown. When cooled, in a plastic bag, shake powdered sugar all over the cookies.

Straight from the Department of Mysteries - these brains have left the tank and have landed on your table!

Melon Brain

1 large watermelon

Directions: Using a carrot peeler, peel away the green rind of watermelon, leaving the inner, white rind. Cut bottom off the melon, to keep it from rolling. Outline squiggling crevices with a toothpick to mimic the furrows of a brain. Using a sharp paring knife, carve along the original tracings, so that some of the inner pink is visible beneath the rind.

Cranberry Bread

2 cups of flour
1 cup of sugar
1 ½ teaspoons of baking powder
1 teaspoon salt (optional)
½ teaspoon of baking soda
¾ cup of orange juice
1 Tablespoon of grated orange peel
2 Tablespoons of butter or margarine
1 egg
1 ½ cups of fresh cranberries, chopped
½ cup of nuts (optional)

Directions: Preheat oven to 350 degrees. In a bowl, mix together the dry ingredients. Pour orange juice, peel, margarine and egg, mix well.

Stir in cranberries and flour. In a greased 9x5 loaf pan, place batter, bake for 40 minutes or until toothpick comes out clean.

Monkey Bread

1 loaf of thawed bread, rolled into balls (frozen bread such as Bridgeford brand)
½ cup (1 stick) of melted butter or margarine
½ cup of sugar and cinnamon mixture

Directions: Roll out balls of thawed bread, and dip them into melted butter. Once dipped in the melted butter, roll them in sugar-cinnamon mixture and layer in a bunt pan. Cook at 350 degrees for 25 minutes or until cooked.

Treacle Crisp

5 cups of sliced peaches
4 tablespoons of granulated sugar
½ cup of rolled oats
½ cup of all-purpose flour
½ cup of light or dark brown sugar
¼ teaspoon of nutmeg, ginger, and/or cinnamon
¼ cup melted margarine
Optional: ¼ cup of coconut or nuts

Directions: Preheat oven to 375 degrees. Melt margarine in the microwave or on the stovetop. Place peaches in a glass or round baking dish. Next, in a mixing bowl, combine oats, brown sugar, flour, and spices. Pour dry mixture over the peaches (the peaches have been placed in either a round or rectangular glass baking dish). Finally, pour melted margarine over the peaches and dry mixture. Bake in a 375 degree oven for 30 minutes, or until fruit is tender and topping is a golden color. Can serve ice cream or whipped cream as a topping to this warm dessert.

Pineapple Platform 9 3/4 to Hogwarts or Hawaii

¼ cup butter or margarine
½ cup brown sugar
1 can sliced pineapple, drained
7 maraschino cherries
6 pecan halves
Cake batter (store bought, follow directions)

Directions: Heat oven to 350 degrees. Melt butter and place in a round layer pan, 9x1-½ inches. Sprinkle brown sugar evenly over butter. Cut and place pineapple slices at the bottom of the pan and arrange. Place the cherries and the pecans around the pineapple slices. Prepare cake batter. Pour evenly over pineapple. Bake 35 to 45 minutes. Cool and then invert onto a plate.

Harry's Tea and Get Out Of a Jam Cookies

2 ½ cups of all-purpose flour
½ teaspoon of baking powder
1 cup margarine or butter, softened
1 egg
1 cup of white sugar
2 teaspoons of vanilla extract
1 cup of your favorite flavor of fruit jam
Makes 4 dozen cookies

Directions: Preheat the oven to 300 degrees. In a bowl, combine flour and baking powder. Mix well and set aside. Next, in a medium sized bowl, cream butter/margarine and sugar, egg, and vanilla extract. Beat with an electric mixer until smooth. Then add the flour mixture and blend on low speed until combined. Roll the dough into 1 inch balls and place on a baking sheet, approximately 1 inch apart. With your thumb, press down the center of the dough balls and shape the ball to form a circle in the middle of the ball. Place a small amount of jam in the center of the dough ball, about ½ of a teaspoon of jam. Bake 20 minutes in a 300 degree oven until golden brown.

Butterbeer Pie

1 carton frozen whipped topping (8 ounces)
1 ready made graham cracker crust
½ cup strawberry jelly
1 cup cold milk

1 package instant butterscotch pudding mix
½ cup of butterscotch chips
½ cup of creamy peanut butter

Directions: Spread 1 cup of the whipped topping over the bottom of the crust. Drop jelly by the tablespoonfuls onto topping. In a bowl, whisk milk and pudding mix until thickened. Add peanut better; mix well. Then, fold in the leftover whipped topping, spread over the jelly and sprinkle with butterscotch chips. Allow to harden in the freezer for at least 4 hours. Serves 6-8.

Easy Butterbeer Drink

8 ounces of ginger ale or cream soda
2 tablespoons of butterscotch syrup

Directions: Mix and serve over ice in a tall glass or mug.

King's Cross Butterscotch Bars

1 cup of all-purpose flour
6 tablespoons of brown sugar
1/8 teaspoon of salt
½ cup of butter or margarine
3 ounces of butterscotch chips
1 tablespoon of Corn syrup
1 tablespoon of Water
2 tablespoons of butter or margarine
1/8 teaspoon of salt
2/3 cup of walnuts, chopped (optional)

Directions: In a bowl, stir together flour, brown sugar, salt and margarine or butter. Next, press the crumbled mixture into an ungreased 9x9 inch pan. Bake in a 375 degree oven for 10 minutes. Next, combine the remaining five ingredients into a saucepan on low heat. Melt mixture and then add the walnuts, if desired. Pour the mixture over the first layer and place back into a 375 degree oven for 8 minutes. Once cooled, cut into squares. Makes approximately 25 Butterscotch bars.

Pumpkin Chocolate Chip Muffins

2 large eggs
½ cup of low fat milk
½ tsp. of vanilla extract
½ cup light brown sugar
1 cup pumpkin
4 tablespoon. margarine, melted
¾ cup heavy cream
½ cup of semi-sweet chocolate chips
½ teaspoon cinnamon
¼ teaspoon salt
¼ teaspoon nutmeg

Directions: Mix all ingredients by hand in a bowl or with a mixer on low speed. Place batter mixture onto a muffin tin and bake at 375 degrees for 15 to 18 minutes.

Halloween Pumpkin Cookies

2 cups of all-purpose flour
½ teaspoon of baking powder
1 teaspoon of vanilla extract
1 teaspoon of cinnamon
¼ cup butter, softened
3/4 cup shortening
1 cup sugar
1 cup pumpkin
½ cup pecans, chopped
½ cup dates, chopped

Directions: Combine all dry ingredients. Next, combine vanilla extract, butter, shortening, sugar, pumpkin and mix until well-blended. Then add ingredients together, add pecans and chopped dates, spoon mixture onto a sprayed cookie sheet and bake at 350 for ten minutes.

Hermiome's Mom's Chocolate Mousse

8 ounces of semi-sweet chocolate chips
2 tablespoons of strong coffee
2 tablespoons of orange extract
1 egg yolk
2 egg whites
A pinch of salt
2 tablespoons of sugar
½ cup heavy cream (or ½ carton of cool whip)

Directions: Melt the chocolate and coffee over low heat. When you remove from heat, add the orange extract and then the egg yolk, stirring till the mixture is smooth. In another bowl, beat the egg whites and salt, next add the sugar and beat it with an electric mixer until stiff peaks from. Lastly, whip the cream until it is stiff and fold into the egg whites and then fold into the chocolate mixture. Place in the refrigerator, chill
Until ready to serve.

Frog's Eye Salad

½ pound package Acinidi Pepe (small round ball pasta)
1 egg
½ cup Sugar
1 15 ounce can crushed pineapple tidbits (drain pineapple and reserve juice)
1 20 ounce can fruit cocktail
1 cup cool whip
1/3 cup of pineapple juice
1 tablespoon of all-purpose flour
¼ teaspoon salt

Directions: Cook Acinidi Pepe according to package directions. Beat egg till foaming in a pan. Then stir in sugar, flour, salt, reserved pineapple liquid, and pineapple juice. Cook over low heat and stir until bubbling. Combine mixture with drained pasta. Cover mixture tightly and allow chilling in the refrigerator overnight. Next day, stir in fruit and cool whip.

Defense Against The Dark Chocolate Chip Cake

1 package of Butter Fudge Cake mix
1 small package of instant vanilla pudding
4 eggs
1 pint of sour cream
¼ cup of chilled strong coffee, such as French or espresso roast
½ cup of oil
8 ounces of chocolate chips

Directions: Mix all ingredients in a bowl with an electric mixer. Place batter into a sprayed bunt pan and bake at 350 degrees for forty minutes. Cool and serve. Once cooled, generously dust top of cake with powdered sugar.

Cockroach Clusters

12 ounces of semi-sweet chocolate chips
Waxed paper
1 teaspoon of grated chocolate or cocoa powder
1 cup of raisins (or a combination of cranberries and raisins)

2 cups of pretzel sticks, broken into one inch pieces.

Directions: In a microwave safe bowl, place chocolate chips in the microwavable bowl and heat for 2 minutes. Stir in raisins, grated chocolate (or cocoa powder) and pretzels. With an ice cream scooper, dollop tablespoonfuls of the mixture onto waxed paper. For a variation to your Cockroach Cluster, try a box of Cracker Jacks, Chow Mein Noodles, and Chocolate chips. Follow same directions as above, but instead of using pretzel sticks and raisins, use Chow Mein Noodles, Cracker Jacks, and raisins. Allow to cool.

Bonbons

¼ cup melted butter
1 can sweetened condensed milk
1 pound powdered sugar
1 package coconut
1 package chocolate chips
½ cube Parowax

Directions: Combine butter, milk, sugar and coconut. Chill at least 30 minutes. Form into small balls and chill again. Melt chocolate chips and wax over hot water. Dip balls into chocolate mixture quickly and remove with fork. Put on waxed paper to cool. Makes 2 dozen bonbons.

Treacle Hot Fudge Sundae

Vanilla ice cream
Fudge
Blanchard almonds
Whipped Cream

Directions: Heat fudge in either a saucepan or in the microwave. Place on top of softened ice cream. Top off with almonds and whipped cream.

Ron and Harry Toasted Marshmallow - as found in the Sorcerer's Stone!

3 tablespoons margarine
1 package regular marshmallows
6 cups of rice crispy cereal

Directions: Melt margarine and marshmallows in the microwave for one minute. Remove from microwave and add the rice crispy cereal and mix with a wooden spoon. Place mixture in a 9x9 inch sprayed pan and mold the rice crisipies with a piece of waxed paper.

Orange Candied Carrots

1 pound of carrots, cut into ½ inch slices
¼ cup of margarine, softened, and cubed
¼ cup of jellied cranberry sauce
1 orange peel strip
2 tablespoon of brown sugar
½ teaspoon salt

Directions: Cook carrots in water in a skillet for 15 to 20 minutes or until crisp and tender. In a blender, combine margarine, cranberry sauce, orange peel, brown sugar and salt. Cover and process until well blended. Drain carrots and drizzle with the cranberry mixture.

Honeydukes Sweet Shop Special

1 cup sifted flour
½ teaspoon salt
1 tablespoon sugar
3 eggs, well beaten
2 cups milk
2 tablespoons melted butter
1 tablespoon cognac
Orangerie sauce:
2   oranges
10 lumps sugar
½ cup softened sweet butter
1   teaspoon lemon juice
¼ cup Grand Marnier
¼ cup cognac
Crepes (3 crepes per person)

Directions: Sift together flour, salt and 1 tablespoon sugar into mixing bowl. Combine eggs, milk, melted butter and 1 tablespoon cognac. Stir in flour mixture. Allow batter to stand 1 hour to improve flavor and texture. Heat a 6-inch crepe pan or skillet and brush the bottom of the pan with melted butter. For each crepe, pour in 2 tablespoons batter. (Spread batter evenly over bottom of pan) Cook, turning once, until nicely browned. Fold crepes into quarters and keep warm.
Wash and dry oranges. Rub sugar lumps over the skin of the orange and then crush lumps into dish. Squeeze juice from oranges into dish. Add butter and lemon juice; cook, stirring constantly, until butter and sugar has melted. Add Grand Marnier and cognac; ignite and quickly pour over crepes.

Wizard

Chocolate or vanilla pastry cream
Puff pastry
1 cup powdered sugar
2 tablespoons water
½ ounce semi-sweet chocolate chips, melted

Directions: Preheat over to 400 degrees. Use a 17 ounce package of frozen puff pastry, let thaw, and then roll out to 12 by 14 inches. Place on a lightly greased cookie sheet and bake according to package directions, then cool. Once the puff pastry has cooled, cut pastry into thirds lengthwise. Mix powdered sugar and water, stir until smooth, until all the lumps of powdered sugar are gone. Pour powdered sugar mixture over one of the pastry strips. With pour chocolate stripes over the glaze and let sit for 30 minutes. With last two pastry strips, spread cream on top. Chill in fridge for one hour until cream is firm. Place all three strips together. Dust with powdered sugar.

Chocolate Pudding

1/3 cup sugar
2   tablespoons cornstarch
1/8 teaspoon salt
2   cups milk
2   egg yolks, slightly beaten
2   tablespoons butter
2   teaspoons vanilla

Directions: Blend sugar, cornstarch and salt in a saucepan (2-quart). Combine milk and egg yolks; gradually stir into sugar mixture. Cook over medium heat, stirring constantly, until it thickens. Boil and stir 1 minute. Remove from heat, stir in butter and vanilla. Serves 4.

Chocolate Bananas

4 bananas
8 popsicle sticks
Magic Shell, any flavor
Wax paper
Toppings: M & M candies, nuts, coconut, chocolate chips.

Directions: Peel and cut bananas in half widthwise. Place Popsicle sticks into each of the 8 banana halves. On a piece of wax paper, place the banana, drizzle with magic shell and add any toppings, if desired. Wrap the banana in the wax paper and place in freezer for 2 hours, or until bananas are frozen. Bananas will be ready for eating and can be kept in freezer for several days.

Licorice Wands

Makes 26 small licorice wands
Takes about one hour to make

1 cup chocolate chip, milk or semi-sweet

13 licorice sticks (your favorite flavor, black or red)

2-3 Oreo or chocolate chip cookies, optional. Place cookies in a plastic sandwich bag and crush them into crumbs, then put in a bowl.

Directions: Cut the licorice sticks in half with cooking scissors. Melt the chocolate chips in a microwave safe bowl by placing microwave on high for 30 seconds. Stir and continue repeating for another 30 seconds until chocolate is melted. Dip the licorice sticks about half-way into the chocolate and sprinkle them with the cookie crumbs as desired. Lastly, place sticks onto wax paper on a plate and set in refrigerator until chocolate is frozen completely.

Luna Lovers Lemon Meringue

Juice of one large lemon and grated rind
1 cup of granulated sugar
2 Tablespoons of butter
3 Tablespoons of corn flour
3 eggs, separated
Pinch of salt
1/8 teaspoon of cream of tartar

Pastry (dough)
1 cup of flour
½ teaspoon of salt
1/3 cup of shortening, cut into pieces

Directions: In a large saucepan, combine the lemon rind and juice, ½ cup of sugar, butter, and 1 cup of water. Bring the mixture to a boil. In a separate medium sized bowl, dissolve the corn flour with 1 Tablespoon of water. Add the egg yolks. Next, add the egg yolks to the lemon mixture and return to a boil, on medium-low heat, stirring continuously until the mixture thickens with a whisk. This will take about five minutes. In order to prevent a skin from forming over the lemon curd mixture, place a piece of waxed paper over the pot. May spray a piece of parchment paper with cooking spray as well. For the meringue, beat the egg whites with salt and cream of tartar with an electric mixer on high until stiff peaks form. Add remaining sugar.

Spoon the lemon curd mixture into the pie shell and spread with a spatula. Spoon the meringue on top, smoothing it up to the edge and create peaks with a spoon. Bake in a 325 degree oven for 10-15 minutes until golden. Serves 8.

For the pastry, sift flour, and salt in a bowl, add the cut pieces of shortening. With a fork and knife, cut into the shortening and flour mixture. Slowly, add in cold tablespoons of water to bind the dough. Add additional flour if needed, gather the dough and make into a dough ball. On a lightly floured surface, roll out the dough. Transfer in a glass pie crust or 9 inch pie tin, and trim the edges with a knife. For the overhang of dough, can fold, crimp the edge or use a fork and make marks as a design around the pie crust.

Halloween Holiday Bark

Orange and black peanut M & M candies
Vanilla chocolate chips, 8 ounce package
2 cups pretzel twists
Wax paper

Directions: Line a cookie sheet with waxed paper. Melt vanilla chips in microwave. Pour melted chips onto waxed paper and spread with a spatula. Next, add peanut m n m's and pretzel twists. Once cooled, break off into pieces.

Wiggle Worm Pie

Foil cupcake liners
Chocolate cookies
Chocolate pudding
Gummy worm candies

Directions: Crush cookies in a plastic bag until they are crumbs. Next, spoon chocolate pudding into a cupcake tin. On top of the chocolate pudding, layer with cookie crumbs and gummy worms. Hint: Quick and easy recipe. May use store bought chocolate pudding or utilize a small box of instant chocolate pudding.

Ghost Pops

Scary, spooky, Ghost Pops. Don't scare your pop with one of these!

White chocolate chips
Banana
Mini chocolate morsels
Raisins
Popcicle sticks
Waxed paper

Directions: Cut banana in half widthwise. Place on a piece of waxed paper. Place a Popsicle stick into each of the halves. Microwave white chocolate chip pieces in a microwave safe bowl for approximately three minutes. Once melted, with a spatula, scoop out the melted chocolate and drizzle over the two banana halves. Then, add raisins and mini chocolate morsels for the eyes and nose of the ghost. Wrap in waxed paper and place in the freezer until firm, about two hours.

Ice Cream Witches

(Makes one ice cream witch)

Wacky Ingredients

1 Sugar Cone (witches hat)
Hardening chocolate syrup (like Magic Shell)
Pistachio or mint chocolate chip ice cream
2 candy coated chocolate pieces (witches eyes)

1 piece of candy corn (witches nose)
1 strand of red licorice (witches mouth)
Small tub of vanilla frosting (to use to stick with)

Directions: Coat inside of a sugar cone with magic shell and place on a thin mint cookie. Place in the freezer on a piece of waxed paper for about twenty minutes or until magic shell has hardened, this will be the witches hat. Place a large scoop of pistachio or mint chocolate chip ice cream on a plate, shape in the form of a ball, (this will be the witches head). With vanilla frosting, coat one side of the 2 chocolate pieces, these will be the eyes. Take the witches eyes, the chocolate pieces, and place the sticky side on the scoop of ice cream. Place a small dollop of frosting on the non pointy side of the candy corn and place on the ice cream scoop to form a nose. Next, take the thin piece of licorice and place in the shape of a mouth, right below the nose. Take witches hat out of the freezer, place on top of the scoop of ice cream. Return ice cream witch to the freezer for five minutes to harden. Serves one.

Midnight Chocolate Cake

2¼ cups flour
12/3 cups sugar
2/3 cup cocoa
1¼ teaspoons soda
1   teaspoon salt
¼   teaspoon baking powder
1¼ cups water
3/4 cup shortening
2   eggs
1   teaspoon vanilla

Directions: Heat oven to 350 degrees. Grease and flour two 9-inch round layer pans. Place all ingredients into a large bowl and blend together with a spoon or with an electric mixer on low speed. Beat 3 minutes on high speed. Take a spatula and scrape the sides and bottom of bowl, make sure all of the ingredients have been mixed well. Pour the batter into greased and floured pans.
Bake for 30-35 minutes or until tooth pick inserted in center comes out clean. Cool. Top with Cloud 9 frosting.

Frosting

½ cup sugar
¼ cup corn syrup
2 tablespoons water
2 egg whites
1 teaspoon vanilla extract

Directions: Place sugar, syrup and water in a saucepan. Cover, and heat to boil over medium heat. As mixture boils, beat egg whites until stiffness forms. Pour mixture from saucepan slowly into the beaten eggs, stirring constantly with electric mixer on medium speed. Add vanilla while beating.

Frothy Champagne Dip

3   eggs
¼   cup of sugar
1   tablespoon finely grated orange peel
2/3 cup of whipping cream
2/3 cup of medium dry champagne
Fresh strawberries

Directions: Place eggs, sugar and orange peel in a small bowl. Set bowl over a pan of simmering water and beat until mixture is thick and fluffy. Remove bowl from heat and beat in whipping cream and champagne. Serve dip with fresh strawberries and slices of lemon or vanilla cake.

Ton Tongue Toffee

2   cups sugar
8   tablespoons of butter
½   teaspoon of vanilla extract
1½ cups water

Directions: In a medium saucepan, mix all ingredients and melt over medium heat until sugar is completely dissolved. With your candy thermometer, boil until the mixture reaches 290 degrees. Pour hot mixture into a greased pan and let cool. A 9 inch x 12 inch pan is preferred. Score the surface of the toffee with a sharp knife when it is cool, and almost firm to the touch. Break toffee into piece and store in a paper bag or wrapped in waxed paper.

Treacle Tart is full of delicious, sweet golden syrup and black treacle. If you can't find golden syrup then use corn syrup. And, likewise, can't find black treacle dark molasses will do.

Creepy Cupcakes

24 baked cupcakes (bake according to package directions)-chocolate cake mix
24 Nutter-Butter (name brand) cookies
Chocolate frosting
Vanilla frosting
Tube of chocolate decorator's icing.

Directions: Frost cupcakes with chocolate frosting. Ice the entire Nutter-Butter cookie with white frosting and use decorator's icing to draw spooky expression on each ghost cookie. Place cookie in the middle of the cupcake. Makes 24 Creepy Cupcakes.

Spooky Spider Cupcakes

1 package of chocolate cake mix
1 package of thin (rope) black licorice
Cup cake liners
Red hot candy

Directions: Follow chocolate cake mix directions and bake cupcakes in cupcake tins. Once cooled, frost with chocolate frosting, and add black licorice for spider legs and two red hot candies for the eyes.

Lemon Scones

2 cups pastry flour
2 tablespoons baking powder
1½ teaspoons fresh lemon peel
1/3 cup granulated sugar
1   egg
½ cup of milk
1   tablespoon vanilla extract
3 tablespoons vegetable oil

Directions: In a large mixing bowl, mix all dry ingredients thoroughly. In a separate bowl, combine all liquids. Add liquids to dry mixture, mixing lightly. Turn out onto floured surface and gently roll out to ¾" thickness. Cut with biscuit cutter and place on lightly oiled baking sheet. Bake at 350 degrees for 15-18 minutes, or until done.

Pumpkin Bread

1 (15 ounce) can pumpkin puree
1 ½ cups of granulated sugar
½ cup vegetable oil
1/4 cup water
2 eggs
2 ¼ cups cups all-purpose flour
1/2 tablespoon ground cinnamon
1/2 tablespoon ground nutmeg
1teaspoons baking soda
1 teaspoons salt
1/2 cup miniature semisweet chocolate chips

Directions Preheat oven to 350 degrees. Grease and flour three 1 pound size coffee cans, or three 9x5 inch loaf pans. In a large bowl, combine sugar, pumpkin, oil, water, and eggs. Beat until smooth. Blend in flour, cinnamon, nutmeg, baking soda, and salt. Fold in chocolate chips and nuts. Fill cans 1/2 to 3/4 full. Bake for

1 hour, or until an inserted knife comes out clean. Cool on wire racks before removing from cans or pans.

Pumpkin Juice

2 tablespoons of pumpkin puree, such as an easy pumpkin pie mix
1 tablespoon of apricot puree, or apricot preserves
1 cup of apple cider (gala apples)
1 cup of apple juice
1 teaspoon of brown sugar

Directions: Place two heaping tablespoons of pumpkin pie mix, 1 tablespoon of apricot preserves, 1 teaspoon of brown sugar, 1 cup of apple cider, 1 cup of apple juice into a food processor and pulse for about 30 seconds.

Witch's Brew

1 14oz. can of sweetened condensed milk
1 46oz. can pineapple juice, chilled
1 2-liter bottle of orange soda, chilled
Orange sherbet ice cream.

Directions: In a punch bowl, or jack o'lantern container, stir together sweetened condensed milk, pineapple juice, and orange soda. Top with sherbet and serve over ice.

Butterbeer

1 cup of Club Soda
½ cup of Butterscotch syrup
½ of a tablespoon of butter

Directions: In a microwave safe bowl, add ½ cup of butterscotch syrup and ½ of a tablespoon of butter and place in the microwave for about one minute until frothy and mixed together. Stir with a spoon and let cool for about thirty seconds. Next, in a large mug pour the club soda and add the slightly cooled butterscotch syrup. It will bubble and enjoy.

Butterbeer Variation

2 scoops of vanilla bean ice cream
2 Tablespoons of butterscotch syrup
1 bottle of cold cream soda

Directions: In a large mug, place scoops of ice cream, add butterscotch syrup and top with a bottle of cold cream soda. The butterbeer will froth.

Hermiome's Precious Potion

1/2 (10-ounce) package frozen raspberries in syrup, thawed
2 cups pineapple juice
1/2 (6-ounce) can frozen lemonade concentrate, thawed
1 bottle (8- ounces) of 7Up
Ice cubcs
Lemon or lime slices for garnish

Directions: In a blender, mix the thawed raspberries, pineapple juice, thawed lemonade, 1- 8 ounce bottle of 7 UP and ice cubes. Mix well, pour into sugar lined margarita glasses and garnish with lemon or lime slices, or both.

Chocolate Covered Frogs

Gummy Frogs
Semi-sweet milk chocolate pieces (can be substituted with white or dark chocolate, depending on your taste)
5   ounces unsweetened pieces, coarsely chopped
2   cups all-purpose flour
2 1/3 teaspoons baking powder
1/4 teaspoon salt
3/8 cup unsalted butter, softened to room temperature
1½ cups of sugar
2   teaspoons vanilla extract
3   large eggs, at room temperature

Directions: Cover a plate with wax paper. This will be used later, after the frogs are dipped. Place chocolate pieces into a microwave safe bowl, and place bowl in microwave. Heat at a medium heat in thirty second intervals, stirring after each one, until the chocolate is completely melted. Be careful not to burn it! Carefully dip the back end of a gummy frog into the chocolate. Place dipped frog onto the wax paper-covered plate. Repeat step 3 with the remaining gummy frogs.
Place the plate of dipped frogs into refrigerator, until the chocolate hardens.

Pumpkin Shake

1 banana, peeled and frozen
3 tablespoons orange juice concentrate
3 tablespoons pumpkin puree
1 scoop vanilla ice cream
$^1/_3$ cup water
Whipped cream
Cinnamon

Directions: Cut frozen banana into small pieces and put all ingredients into blender. Blend on high until smooth, pour into tall glasses and top with whipped cream and cinnamon.

Bertie Bott's Every Flavor Beans

baked bean
booger
chocolate
coconut
coffee
curry
ear wax
grass
liver
pepper
peppermint
sardine
spinach
sprouts
strawberry
toast
toffee
vomit

Easy Butterbeer Cupcakes

1 box Yellow Cake mix
1 box Instant Butterscotch Pudding
1 teaspoon baking soda
1 cup Buttermilk
½ cup oil
4 eggs

1 pint heavy whipping cream
1½ cup powdered sugar
1 tablespoon of butter
1 tablespoon of vanilla extract
1 tablespoon of caramel (Ice Cream Topping)

Directions: Preheat oven to 350F. Line the bottom of cupcake tins with paper liners. In a mixing bowl, mix together the yellow cake mix, instant butterscotch pudding mix and baking soda. Add in buttermilk, oil and eggs and stir with electric mixer until smooth. Fill each cupcake tin and bake for 12 minutes or until a toothpick inserted in middle comes out clean. Cool at room temperature. In a separate mixing bowl, whip up heavy whipping cream until it begins to make peaks.
Add the powdered sugar, butter, vanilla extract, and caramel and continue whipping until well blended.

Cauldron Cakes

3/4 cups flour
½ cup of cocoa powder

½ teaspoon of baking powder
1 teaspoon of baking soda
¼ teaspoon of salt
1 cup of soy milk
1 teaspoon of apple cider vinegar
1/3 cup of canola oil
1 cup sugar
1 teaspoon vanilla extract
1 cup of chocolate chunks
Cocoa powder

Preheat oven to 375 degrees. In a large bowl, combine flour, cocoa powder, baking powder, baking soda, salt, and whisk all of the dry ingredients together. In separate bowl, (¾ cup) soy milk, apple cider vinegar (let stand for a minute as to curdle the milk), next add canola oil, sugar, vanilla extract and whisk together. Place wet ingredients over dry ingredients and whisk again for two minutes or for about 1 minute with an electric mixer. In a greased cupcake pan (or mini Bundt pan), add the batter and place in the preheated oven for about 15 minutes, be sure not to overcook. Place a toothpick in the center of the cupcake. If the toothpick comes out clean, then the cupcake is ready.

Melt together 1 cup of chocolate chunks and (¼ cup) soy milk to make a quick ganache and spread over the tops of the caldrons and sprinkle with cocoa powder.

Cream Puffs

2 (3.5 ounce) packages of instant vanilla pudding mix
2 cups of heavy whipping cream
1 cup of milk
½ cup of butter
1 cup of water
¼ teaspoon of salt
1 cup of flour
4 medium sized eggs

Directions: Preheat oven to 425 degrees. In a bowl, mix together pudding mix, cream and milk. Keep in the refrigerator and cover. In a large pot, bring water and butter to a rolling boil. Stir in flour and salt until the mixture forms a ball. Transfer the dough to a large mixing bowl. Use a wooden spoon and beat the eggs one at a time. Drop the dough by tablespoonfuls and bake for 20 minutes until golden brown. When the shells are cool, split the centers with a knife, and fill with the pudding mixture, place top back on cream puff and with a sifter polish with powdered sugar.

Yorkshire Pudding

Yorkshire Pudding is mentioned in Harry Potter books as the traditional dessert of England. This is traditionally served at the family Sunday Dinner, along with roast meat, veggies and potatoes.

½ pound of flour
1/4 teaspoon salt
2 eggs
1 pint cream
2 tablespoons bacon fat

Directions: Mix flour and salt in a bowl, and form a depression in its center. Break the eggs and pour them into the center of this. Slowly add the cream, mixing as you go. Let the mix stand for 1/2 hour. Divide the drippings up into 8 muffin tins. Heat these in a 425F oven until they smoke, 5-10 minutes. Pour in the batter and leave in a few minutes until it browns. Then drop the heat to 375F and cook for 15 minutes.

Chocolate and Apricot Torte
- of Little Hangleton Village

½ cup of unsalted butter
1 cup of semi-sweet chocolate chips
5 large eggs, separated
3/4 cup of sugar
1 cup ground Almonds
1/3 cup dried apricots, finely chopped
Dried apricots and fresh strawberries for garnish

Directions: Melt chocolate chips and butter together in the top of a double boiler and cool. Beat the egg yolks with the sugar until they become pale yellow. Mix the cooled chocolate mixture into the eggs and sugar mixture, blending in the ground nuts. Add the chopped apricots too. Next, beat the egg whites until stiff, and fold into the chocolate mixture. Place a pan of water on the bottom shelf of a pre-heated 375 degrees oven*. Finally, line the bottom and side of a 9 inch spring form pan with aluminum foil and place Pam cooking spray on the aluminum foil. Pour in the batter and bake for 45 to 50 minutes. Remove from the oven and cool in the pan for 15 minutes Release the sides of the pan and carefully place onto a serving plate. Peel off the foil and allow to cool completely. To serve, dust with ground almonds or powdered sugar. Garnish with strawberry halves and apricots.

*Placing a pan of water on the bottom shelf helps make the torte moist.

Ron's Love Spell Cookies

1 cup butter
¼ cup milk
1 teaspoon vanilla
4 cups flour
2 eggs
1 ½ cups granulated sugar
1 teaspoon baking soda

Directions: Cut butter into flour. Combine sugar, eggs, milk, and vanilla. Mix all ingredients together. Roll out the dough onto a floured surface ¼ inch in thickness. Cut with a heart shaped cookie cutter. Place on a baking sheet. Bake at 350° for 8 to 10 minutes. Yields 3 dozen cookies.

Mulled Mead

1 quart of water
1 cup of honey
1/2 teaspoon of nutmeg
1/4 teaspoon of ginger
1/2 teaspoon almond extract

Directions: Add all ingredients to a pan, and bring to a boil on the stove. As it begins to boil, a skin will form on the surface. Scrape it off, and continue to stir the contents of the pan until the scum ceases to form. Allow for time to cool.

Main Dishes

Dinner In a Skillet

½ Tablespoon of vegetable oil
1   Tablespoon of sugar
1   Pound of lean hamburger
2 Teaspoons of minced garlic
1 Medium onion, diced
1 Medium head of cabbage, shredded or cut into slightly larger than bite size pieces.
1 Can of tomato soup
1 Can (8 ounces) of tomato sauce
¼ Cup of water
Optional- 1 Tablespoon of soy sauce and 1 teaspoon of salt

Directions: In a skillet, add 1/2 Tablespoon of vegetable oil. Next,
add 1 Tablespoon of sugar and immediately add the hamburger meat, onion, and minced garlic. Cook

uncovered over low heat, checking on the meat until browned and using a spatula to break the hamburger meat up into smaller pieces. Once the hamburger meat is browned, you can take it off the stove top and remove the excess fat by scooping the hamburger meat over a plate lined with paper towels. The paper towels will absorb the excess fat. Wash the skillet out with lukewarm water and place the meat with garlic and onion back in the skillet and add the cabbage, tomato soup and tomato sauce (may add salt and soy sauce). Cook covered on low heat until cabbage is tender about 20 minutes. Makes 6 to 8 servings and may serve with white or brown rice.

Oriental Style Fried Rice

2 Tablespoon. vegetable oil
1 Teaspoon salt
1 Onion, finely diced
2 Eggs, beaten
1 Celery stalk, finely chopped
1 Cup frozen peas and carrots
1 Cup bean sprouts
6 Cups cooked white rice
3 Tablespoon soy sauce
2 Scallions, green onions (the green part), sliced

Directions: Cook rice according to package directions. Heat oil in a large non-stick frying pan or wok. Add salt and onion, stirring until tender. Add celery. Then, stir in eggs and keep cooking till eggs are done. Then, add in the frozen peas and carrots and cover and simmer for five minutes over low heat. Remove the lid and add the rice, scallions and soy sauce.

Chicken Skewers

Skinless boneless Chicken breasts, washed, and cut into large cubes
Skinned and washed Russet Potatoes, cut 1 potato into quarters
Red onion, cut into large pieces
Skewers.
MEDIUM

Directions: Place chicken cubes, potato quarters, red onion and green and red pepper onto a skewer and alternating pieces. Place on a low barbeque and cook slowly, trying not to burn. When chicken is no longer pink in the middle, your skewers are ready.

Conjure up some...

Christmas Coconut Soup

1 Cup of chicken broth
1 Can, 13.5 ounces of coconut milk
1 Can, 15 ounces of stir-fry vegetables, mushrooms,
water chestnuts, bean sprouts, and bamboo shoots
1 Lime
1 Teaspoon of sugar
Cilantro springs
Roasted chicken, cubed
Shrimp (optional)
MEDIUM

Directions: In a large pot, place chicken broth, coconut milk, juice of a lime, 1 Teaspoon of sugar, cubed chicken, whole divined shrimp and cook on medium low for ten minutes.

Corned Beef and Cabbage

4   Pounds of corned beef
1   Teaspoon oil
2   Celery stocks, chopped
1   Onion, diced
2   Cloves of garlic, minced
2   Tablespoon of dried thyme
¼ Cup of whiskey
1   Teaspoon black pepper
2   Bay leaves
1   Cabbage, cut into wedges
2   Tablespoon. honey mustard
1   Teaspoon parsley
MEDIUM

Directions: Place all ingredients, except cabbage into a crock pot. Add water if needed. Cook for 7 to 10 hours, or until meat is fully cooked. On the stove top, place a pot with water and cabbage wedges. Cook until cabbage is wilted. Serve hot on a platter along with the corned beef.

Easy Corned Beef and Cabbage

4   Pounds corned beef
1   Large head of cabbage

Olive Oil and vinegar
EASY

Directions: Cover meat with cold water and simmer for
3 hours. Add cut cabbage and cook until tender. Season
with olive oil and vinegar. Serves 8. Can also place the
corned beef into a crock-pot and slow cook for 6 hours.

"With every job, you're typically looking for the director to make sure you're
doing the right thing but with Emma, Rupert and Daniel, that has become part of
their psyche. They've been doing that job so long, they have such ease and an
instant connection with it, and a real truthfulness."- Ciaran Hinds, the actor who
will play Aberforth Dumbledore in Deathly Hallows Part 2.

Corned Beef Sandwich

2 Slices bread
Softened butter
2 Slices cooked corned beef
 Mustard, such as Dijon or regular Yellow Mustard

Directions: Spread bread with butter and mustard.
Place corned beef in the middle of the two bread slices
and add the corned beef. Cut sandwich in half and serve
with a pickle or a side of potato salad.

Fun Fact: There are a number of different types of mustard which are cultivated
for different products, including greens and leaves. The diversity of the mustard
plants and types, French mustard such as Dijon and black mustard seeds made
mustard a flavor put in American Southern or traditional Irish and English
dishes.

Potter Stew

2 1/2 Cups water
1 1/2 Pounds cooked lamb, diced
1   Teaspoon salt
1/4 Teaspoon pepper
2 Small onions, sliced
1 Turnip, diced
2 Medium sized carrots, diced
1 Celery stalk, diced
2 Cups cubed potatoes

Directions: Place enough water to cover meat in a pot; add onions, turnip, carrots, celery, and potatoes and cook 35 to 40 minutes. Thicken liquid with flour if necessary and serve stew with dumplings.

Fun Facts About England:
A clever Frenchman opened London's first hot chocolate store in the mid 1600's. By the early 1700's hot chocolate stores were just as popular as coffee stands.

Dumbledore's Delightful Dumplings

2 Cups sifted flour
1 1/4 Teaspoons baking powder
3/4 Teaspoon salt
1 Tablespoon butter
2/3 Cup of milk

Directions: Sift dry ingredients together. Cut in butter. Add milk to make soft dough. Roll 1/2 inch thick on a floured board. Cut into squares, and drop in hot oil, cook 20 minutes. Makes 10 dumplings.

Fun Facts About England:
The English drink more tea per person than any other country in the world. They drink twenty times more tea per person than an American.

England has one of the oldest working monarchies and at date of this publication, Prince William will be marrying in April 2011 and his grandmother, Queen Elizabeth II is queen of England.

Hagrid's Hearty Potatoes au gratin

4 Cups chopped white potatoes
¼ Cup low-fat milk
Minced garlic
2 Tablespoons cream cheese or grated cheddar cheese
½ Teaspoon salt
1/8 Teaspoon pepper
1 Can of black beans, drained

Directions: Cut and peel potatoes and place in a saucepan with water. Bring to a boil, and reduce the heat to low. Cook for 20 minutes, or until soft. Once the potatoes are cooked, drain the water and add milk, garlic, cream cheese, salt and pepper. Mash the ingredients with an electric mixer. Once the lumps are out, place potatoes in a pastry bag and squeeze the mashed potatoes onto a lightly buttered cookie sheet. Squeeze in such a way as to resemble ghosts, then place two black beans for eyes. Bake for 5 minutes in a preheated 350 degree oven.

Pasta with Creamy Garlic and Walnut Sauce

1 ½ Cups of heavy cream
1   Cup of walnuts or candied walnuts*
¾ Cup of shredded romano cheese
2 Garlic cloves, peeled
1 Teaspoon of salt
½ Teaspoon of ground black pepper
1 Pound of bow tie shaped pasta
Serves 6

Directions: Place cream, walnuts, cheese, salt and pepper and garlic into a food processor and blend until mixture is smooth. Cook pasta according to the package directions, and drain. Toss pasta with the sauce and return to a pan to heat the sauce. May garnish with cilantro and additional walnuts.

*Candied walnuts make the pasta have a little sweet kick.

Pasta with Roasted Red Peppers and Spinach

2 ¼ Cups of Rotelle or Mostaccioli Pasta
½ Pound of Sweet Italian Sausage, cut into ¼ inch slices
1 Small purple or yellow onion, chopped
2 Cloves of garlic, minced
1 Can of Italian Stewed Tomatoes, (16 ounces)
1 Red Pepper, cut lengthwise into strips
3 Cups of Fresh Spinach or 1 (10 ounce) package green spinach, thawed
Parmesan Cheese to taste

Directions: Cook pasta according to package directions. In a skillet, add olive oil, onion, cut sausage, minced garlic, red pepper and cook sausage until browned. Place on low heat and add stewed tomatoes, about ¼ cup of water and spinach and cook until spinach is wilted and stewed tomatoes are warm. Place all ingredients in a bowl with the fresh cooked pasta, toss, and add parmesan cheese to taste.

Pasta with Broccoli and Artichokes

1 Pound of bow tie pasta
Fresh broccoli, washed and halved

8-10 Pepperoni, cut into 1 inch slivers
1 Jar artichoke hearts,
½ Cup of sun dried tomatoes, cut into fourth with cooking scissors
3 Green onions, diced
1 Tablespoon of red-wine vinegar
¼ Teaspoon of salt and pepper
¼ Cup of parmesan cheese

Directions: In a large pot, bring 4 to 6 quarts of water to a rolling boil, add a little salt or about a teaspoon of olive oil to the water, if desired. Next, add bow tie pasta to the boiling water, stir gently, boil uncovered for 7 minutes, then add broccoli and cook for an additional 5 minutes. For more "al dente" pasta, reduce cooking time from 12 minutes to 9 minutes. Remove from heat, and drain. In a bowl, add cooked pasta, broccoli, and the other ingredients, the pepperoni slivers, diced artichoke hearts, cut sun dried tomatoes, diced green onions, and the red-wine vinegar as well as the parmesan cheese. May add more parmesan cheese if desired for flavoring and salt and pepper to taste. May serve Pasta with Broccoli and Artichokes hot or chilled. 440 calories per serving, serves 6.

Tallerina

3 Tablespoons shortening
1 Onion, minced
1 Pound ground round
1 Cans tomato soup
1 15 Ounce can tomato sauce
1 Cup cold water
2 Tablespoons salt
2 Cups uncooked broad egg noodles
2 Cups of whole grain canned corn
1 Can ripe pitted olives
1 Cup grated cheddar cheese
1 Can mushrooms

Directions: Melt shortening in a large pot, add onions
and cook until brown. Next, add meat and brown; then
add tomato soup, tomato sauce, noodles, water, and salt.
Cover and cook over low heat for 10 minutes. Remove

pot from stove and add corn, mushrooms, and part of the cheddar cheese and mix. Pour entire mixture into a baking dish; cover with remaining cheese and bake at 350 degrees for 50 minutes.

Hogwarts Best Bruscetta

(Liz Longo creation)

4 Sausages, hot or sweet
2 Cups of mushrooms
1 Loaf of Italian Bread
2 Cloves of Garlic, minced
1 Cup Olive Oil
1 Pound of fresh Mozzarella cheese
A dash of oregano
A dash of basil
6-8 Cherry tomatoes

Directions: Cook sausage to almost perfection in your favorite oil, oregano and garlic, add mushrooms and simmer. Slice Italian bread in four then separate top and bottom and align on a baking sheet. Drizzle olive oil over bread. Press garlic to spread over oil on bread. Once mushrooms and sausage are equally perfected, dice in bite size pieces and layer on top of bread. Sprinkle oregano. Slice your mozzarella and layer on top of sausage and mushrooms. Cut cherry tomatoes in half and place on top of the mozzarella. Place in the oven at 350-degrees for 10 minutes until mozzarella is melted to desired consistency. Dip fresh basil into your favorite and uncooked olive oil, allow to excess to drip for a few moments and set the by tomatoes to top it all off. Serve warm.

Lasagna

1 Container, 15 ounces of ricotta cheese
1 Egg
1 Package, 8 ounces of shredded mozzarella cheese, and 1/3 cup parmesan cheese
1 Jar, 28 ounces of Spaghetti Sauce
1 Can of tomato sauce, 8 ounces
½ of a 16 ounce box of uncooked lasagna noodles.
Optional: 1 box of frozen chopped spinach, 1 cup of sliced mushrooms, or 1 cup shredded zucchini
Spices to season with: basil, oregano, garlic, parsley, and fenugreek.

Directions: Preheat oven to 350 degrees. Combine ricotta cheese, egg, and parmesan-mozzarella cheese combination as well as the seasonings in a bowl, mix well. Next, spray the bottom of a 9 x 13 inch pan and place part of the cooked lasagna noodles. Once the noodles are in the pan, start layering with the ricotta mixture, spaghetti sauce, tomato sauce, and remaining noodles. (May add optional ingredients at this time as well). Cover with aluminum foil and bake for 75 minutes in a 350 degree oven. Allow to cool 10 to 15 minutes before serving.

Chicken Cacciatore

1- 3 Pound whole fryer chicken, cut into pieces and washed
½ Cup of oil
Garlic salt to taste
2 Tablespoons of chopped parsley
1 Clove of garlic
Pinch of thyme
2 Leaves of sage
1 Sprig of rosemary
1 Small can of Italian stewed tomatoes, chopped
1 Small can of tomato sauce
1 Can of button mushroom, drain

Directions: Cut and wash chicken pieces. In a deep
frying pan, place oil and cut pieces of chicken, sprinkle
with garlic salt and cook until chicken has browned.
Once the chicken has browned, add the herbs and spices

as well as the tomato sauce, chopped tomatoes, and mushrooms. Cook on high heat for thirty minutes.

Banoffi Inspired...
Pizza Pie

1 Cup Marinara Sauce
1 Cup shredded mozzarella cheese
1/4 Teaspoon dried oregano
2 Tablespoons grated Parmesan cheese

Directions: Preheat oven to 450 degrees. Prepare pizza dough. Spread marinara sauce over the dough, then sprinkle with mozzarella cheese, oregano, and Parmesan cheese. Bake pizza for 30 minutes or until crust is well browned.

Dough

Makes 3-12 inch pizzas
1 Envelope of dry yeast
2 Cups lukewarm water
4 Cups flour
1/2 Tablespoon of sugar
1/2 Tablespoon of salt
1/8 Cup of olive oil

Directions: In a small bowl empty contents of yeast package and add 1/4 cup of lukewarm water and stir until the yeast is dissolved. Set aside until the yeast starts forming bubbles, in about five minutes. Next, in a larger bowl, add yeast and lukewarm water with the dry ingredients and as much as the remaining warm water that is needed. Add the olive oil and stir mixture with a spatula. Mix with your hands to form the dough. You may want to spray your hands with cooking spray to assist in making the dough not stick to your hands. Sprinkle some flour on a wooden surface. Knead the dough with your hands, pushing, and folding. Return the dough back to a bowl back that is slightly oiled (with either olive oil or cooking spray) and cover with a clean kitchen cloth. Allow dough to rise until dough doubles in size, approximately 1 ½ hours. Return to the same work surface, and cut the dough into two or three equal pieces (depending on how many pizzas you are planning to make, the more pizzas the thinner the crust will turn out) with a rolling pin, on the floured surface, make desired shape. Can create a circular or a square style dough. Return dough to an oiled round pizza pan or a cookie sheet (if making a rectangular shaped pizza).

Create Your Own...
Perfect Little Pizza

English Muffins
Pizza or spaghetti sauce
Mozzarella cheese
Pineapple chunks
Pepperoni
Black olives
Green pepper
Fresh sliced mushrooms

Directions: Slice all of the ingredients into bite sized pieces. Grate the mozzarella cheese and place the pizza or spaghetti sauce on an English muffin. After the sauce is on the muffin, add cheese and your favorite toppings. Place the pizza on a cookie sheet and bake at 350 degrees for 6 minutes or until cheese is melted.

About the Author

Gina Meyers is best known for her popular culture television trivia and cooking expertise books related to the Twilight Saga and the iconic television show *Bewitched*. Gina's *Love at First Bite: the Unofficial Twilight Cookbook*, first edition, has been listed in *OK!* magazine's top *Twilight* merchandise must-haves and featured on Comedian Alan Carr, Chatty Man's late night show out of England.

Gina's *Magic of Bewitched* trivia books and cookbooks have sold over 3,000 copies internationally, and she was featured as the top *Bewitched* expert on the television show documentary *Fanatical*. Her books have been given the nose up (twitch) from famed director of *Bewitched*, William Asher.

The Unofficial Harry Potter Cookbook: From Rock Cakes to Butterbeer came as magically as her passion for cooking and creating unique themed recipes. Gina's goal is to share her love of cooking and creating with people from all over the globe and to reignite a spark of imagination.

Gina has been a television consultant for *Popstar! Magazine* and Columbia Pictures Television, as well as *Nickelodeon Magazine*. She is a featured business expert at business.com and is the *San Jose Cooking Examiner*. Gina has worked for Google as well as Xerox Corporation. Ms. Meyers is married and resides in Central California with her husband David and their two children.

Index:

Acknowledgements:

Creating a book is one of those truly unusual, unique, fun and magical experiences. A book is never the work of just one person, it takes a team of hopeful, responsible, caring individuals who devote time, photography skills, moral support, experience, effort, loyalty and devotion. Thank you to my husband David, daughter Lauren, and son Lucas for always believing in my projects. Thank you Lauren for spending most of your thanksgiving break taking awesome photographs for this Unofficial Harry Potter Cookbook and our future ventures. Thank you Lucas for your enthusiasm and assistance in cooking in the kitchen, specifically, your awesome pumpkin degutting and pureeing.

A very special thank you to artist, author, and friend, Liz Longo who has a keen sense for detail, a Brooklyn bluntness that I understand and appreciate, a motherly instinct that transfers to this cookbook project, and a love for the Harry Potter series. Thank you to Harry Potter fans who are looking to reignite a passion for cooking unique themed recipes.

A cookbook also is a special artistic form that is such a difficult task to complete, like the recipes found in this cookbook, when they are created, aka baked, eaten, and enjoyed, one gets a brief glimpse of the challenge of writing the recipes. I am eternally grateful to J.K. Rowling for continuing to hope and aspire to bring her characters' to life, despite the sacrifice, hardship, blood, sweat, toil and tears that she had to endure until someone believed in her project. A few months ago, on our way to Burbank, California (for a Hollywood Collector's Show to meet Barbara Eden), I called the Marriott hotel to confirm our reservation. A lady (aka an angel) by the name of May, said to me in a jovial manner, "Right before you called, I was thinking about the lady who wrote Harry Potter and how she was poor and then became rich, I wish this for you." The truly strange part is I hadn't even thought of writing an Unofficial Harry Potter Cookbook until a few days after that conversation. Thank you May! Visit our Unofficial Harry Potter Cookbook blog site: http://unofficialhpcookbook.blogspot.com/

Serendipity Media specializes in cookbooks, inspirational, poetry, popular culture, how- to, and trivia books.
www.serendipitymediagroup@gmail.com

For Immediate Release:
A Bird and Its Albatross, a Tale of Renewal
ISBN: *978-0-9825039-4-2*
Author: Liz Longo
Publisher: Serendipity Media
Retail Price: $18.95
Full color, 8x10
Category: Inspiration, Poetry

A time ago in wondrous Australia, there lived a very beautiful yet melancholy bird. He lived in a dense old tree beside a river. All day, the Silver-tailed Cockatiel sat as still as steel. But in the evening, he would leap along from branch to branch trying to settle in for the night. His thoughts were as deep as the night sky...

"A bird flies and so too our thoughts..." In common, they seemingly fly aimlessly yet eventually land. – Author and poet, Liz Longo

9 780982 503959